THE CULTURE
IN PICTURES

PUNK! THE CULTURE IN PICTURES

First published 2012 by
Ammonite Press
an imprint of AE Publications Ltd,
166 High Street, Lewes, East Sussex, BN7 1XU

ISBN 978-1-90770-829-9

British Cataloguing in Publication Data. A catalogue record of this book is available from the British Library.

Editor: Ian Penberthy
Series Editor: Richard Wiles
Picture research: Mirrorpix
Design: Gravemaker + Scott

Colour reproduction by GMC Reprographics
Printed and bound in China by C&C Offset Printing Co. Ltd

Idol talk
Page 2: Billy Idol (real name William Broad) came to prominence as a member of the punk band Generation X. Inspiration for his stage name came from his school days, when a teacher described him as "idle".
11th September, 1984

Style points
Page 5: Hair that was deliberately made to look messy or dyed unnatural colours, leather jackets, studs and chains were all part of the look adopted by many punks.
3rd February, 1980

Shock tactics
Page 6: Punks reinforced their anti-establishment stance by creating a look that was intended to shock and unsettle. Some took it to extremes with facial piercings, make-up and outlandish hair.
3rd February, 1980

THE

Sex Pistols
I'M A MESS
ANARCHY IN

Introduction

Punk rock developed in the UK, the USA and Australia during the mid-1970s as a grass-roots reaction to the perceived excesses and pretensions of disco and mainstream rock. Punk bands played fast, hard-edged music, typically with basic instrumentation and often anti-establishment lyrics. Their short songs, backed by distorted guitars and loud drumming, drew heavily on 1960s garage rock and 1970s pub rock.

Bands such as The Ramones in New York, and The Sex Pistols and The Clash in London were the forerunners of this new musical movement, which would soon spread around the world. A punk sub-culture emerged, with an anti-establishment, anti-capitalist ethos, and characterised by distinctive clothing and accessories. The latter was designed to make a non-conformist, provocative statement, and included spiked and studded leather jackets and chokers, chain belts, heavy boots, ripped T-shirts (often bearing hand-written anarchic or offensive slogans and held together with safety pins), rubber and leather fetishwear, 'drainpipe' jeans and bondage trousers with their legs joined by long straps. Some punks made a point of wearing dirty, secondhand clothes as a stand against consumerism.

Many punks wore unkempt, short hair, but bright, unnatural colours became popular, as did styling the hair into startling shapes, including tall spikes and the famed Mohican, or Mohawk, crop. Tattoos and piercings complemented the look.

Much of punk fashion in the UK was inspired by Sex Pistols manager Malcolm McLaren and his partner, designer Vivienne Westwood. In addition, a group of Pistols fans from Kent, known as the Bromley Contingent, among them Susan Ballion (Siouxsie Sioux) and William Broad (Billy Idol), were early trend setters.

By the early 1980s, faster and more aggressive forms of punk rock, such as hardcore punk and Oi!, had become prominent. Musicians whose roots were in punk, or who had been inspired by it, also pursued other variations, leading to post-punk, New Wave and the alternative rock movement. By the turn of the century, pop punk had gone mainstream, bands such as America's Green Day and Britain's McFly achieving widespread popularity for the genre.

Looking out for teds

A group of punks on the King's Road in London, where clashes took place with gangs of teddy boys.
30th July, 1977

Once a teddy boy. . Manager of the Sex Pistols, Malcolm McLaren, in the days before punk, when he was a teddy boy with a shop called Let it Rock on the King's Road, Chelsea.
14th March, 1972

Boys in the band
Seminal punk band the Sex Pistols. L–R: Glen Matlock, Johnny Rotten, Steve Jones, Paul Cook.
2nd December, 1976

Strange boy
Singer Steve Strange (above second R and far R) with punk friends.
1976

Doll faces
American glam rock band the New York Dolls were credited with having a major influence on the sound of early punk bands on both sides of the Atlantic.
11th November, 1973

The look
Left: Punk fashion defined by black jacket and bondage trousers; dyed black hair.
1977

The Godmother

Known as the 'Godmother of punk', American singer/songwriter Patti Smith was very influential on the New York scene.

10th May, 1975

Followers of fashion

Blazers, studded chokers, leather trousers and fishnets – a kaleidoscope of punk fashion.

1976

Bowie men

This punk trio clearly owe their allegiance to Ziggy Stardust. Swastika emblems were worn to shock rather than suggest support of extreme right-wing politics.

1976

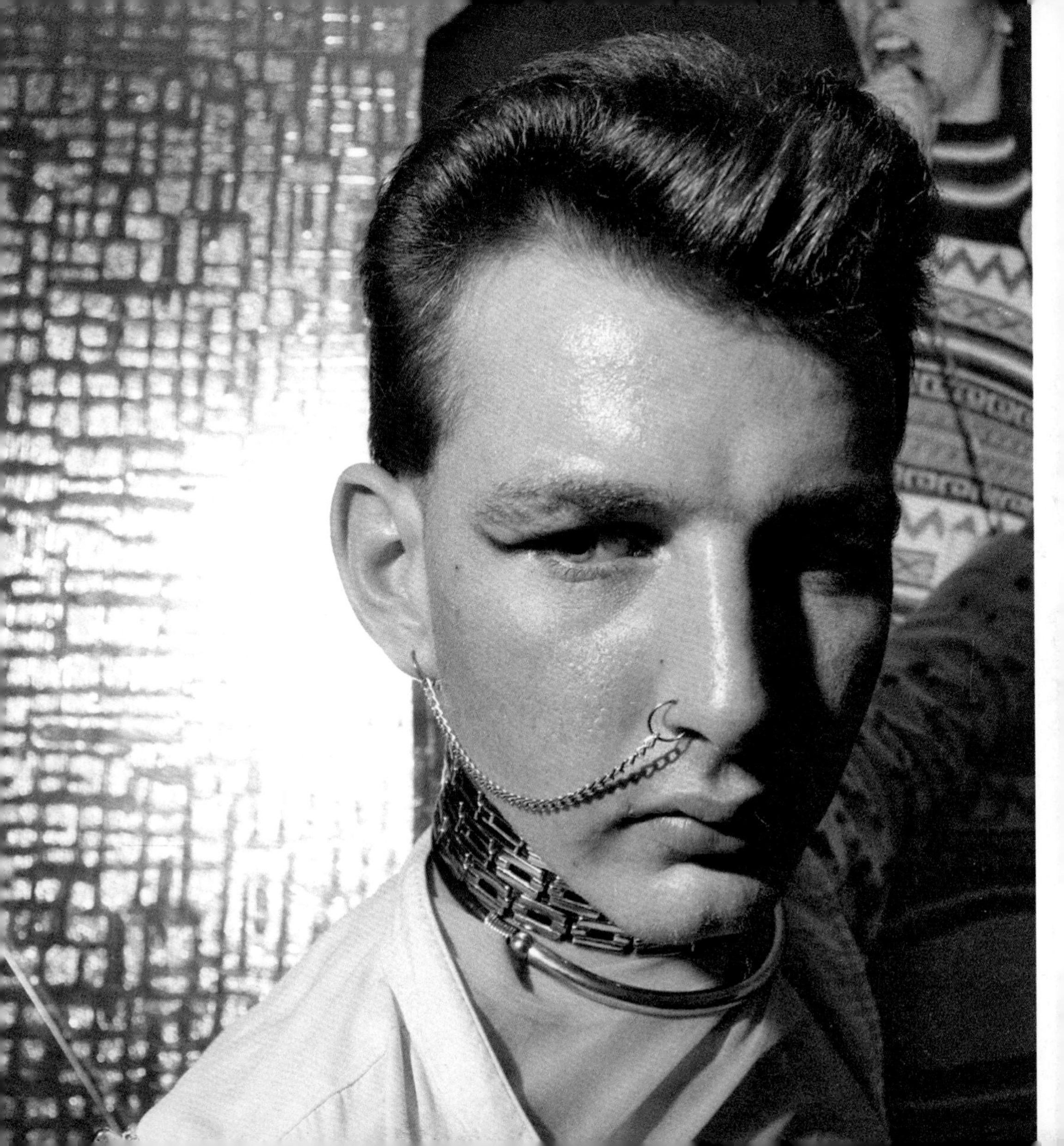

Going Global

Punks at The Global village disco. The essence of diy punk style: accessorise with safety pins and chains, or try a little face painting.

20th November, 1976

ɔaily ɪirror

AIN'S BIGGEST DAILY SALE

y, December 2, 1976 • No. 22,658

TV's Bill Grundy in rock outrage

THE GROUP IN THE BIG TV RUMPUS

Johnny Rotten, leader of the Sex Pistols, opens a can of beer. Last night their language made TV viewers froth.

THE FILTH AND THE FURY!

When the air turned blue . .

INTERVIEWER Bill Grundy introduced the Sex Pistols to viewers with the comment: "Words actually fail me about the next guests on tonight's show."

The group sang a number — and the amazing interview got under way.

GRUNDY: I am told you have received £40,000 from a record company. Doesn't that seem to be slightly opposed to an anti-materialistic way of life.

PISTOL: The more the merrier.

GRUNDY: Really.

PISTOL: Yea, yea.

GRUNDY: Tell me more then.

PISTOL: F——ing spent it, didn't we.

GRUNDY: You are serious?

PISTOL: Mmmm.

GRUNDY: Beethoven, Mozart, Bach?

PISTOL: They're wonderful people.

GRUNDY: Are they?

PISTOL: Yes they really turn us on. They do.

GRUNDY: Suppose they turn other people on?

PISTOL (in a whisper): That's just their tough s——.

GRUNDY: It's what?

PISTOL: Nothing—a rude word. Next question.

GRUNDY: No, no. What was the rude word?

PISTOL: S——.

GRUNDY: Was it really? Good heavens. What about you girls behind? Are you married or just enjoying yourself?

GIRL: I've always wanted to meet you.

GRUNDY: Did you really? We'll meet afterwards, shall we?

PISTOL: You dirty old man. You dirty old man.

GRUNDY: Go on, you've got another long time yet. You've got another five seconds. Say something outrageous.

PISTOL: You dirty sod. You dirty bastard.

GRUNDY: Go on. Again.

PISTOL: You dirty f——er.

GRUNDY: What?

PISTOL: What a f——ing rotter.

GRUNDY: Well, that's it for tonight . . . I'll be seeing you soon. I hope I'm not seeing YOU again. Goodnight.

A POP group shocked millions of viewers last night with the filthiest language heard on British television.

The Sex Pistols, leaders of the new "punk rock" cult, hurled a string of four-letter obscenities at interviewer Bill Grundy on Thames TV's family teatime programme "Today".

The Thames switchboard was flooded with protests.

Nearly 200 angry viewers telephoned the Mirror. One man was so furious that he kicked in the screen of his £380 colour TV.

Grundy was immediately carpeted by his boss and will apologise in tonight's programme.

Shocker

A Thames spokesman said: "Because the programme was live, we could not foresee the language which would be used. We apologise to all viewers."

The show, screened at peak children's viewing time, turned into a shocker when Grundy asked about £40,000 that the Sex Pistols received from their record company.

By STUART GREIG, MICHAEL McCARTHY and JOHN PEACOCK

One member of the group said: "F---ing spent it, didn't we?"

Then when Grundy asked about people who preferred Beethoven, Mozart and Bach, another Sex Pistol remarked: "That's just their tough s---."

Later Grundy told the group: "Say something outrageous."

A punk rocker replied: "You dirty sod. You dirty bastard."

"Go on. Again," said Grundy.

"You *dirty f---er.*"

"What?"

Uproar as viewers jam phones

"What a f---ing rotter."

As the Thames switchboard became jammed, viewers rang the Mirror to voice their complaints.

Lorry driver James Holmes, 47, was outraged that his eight-year-old son Lee heard the swearing . . . and kicked in the screen of his TV.

"It blew up and I was knocked backwards," he said. "But I was so angry and disgusted with this filth that I took a swing with my boot.

"I can swear as well as anyone, but I don't want this sort of muck coming into my home at teatime."

Mr. Holmes, of Beechfield Walk, Waltham Abbey, Essex, added: "I am not a violent person, but I would like to have got hold of Grundy.

"He should be sacked for encouraging this sort of disgusting behaviour."

WHO ARE THESE PUNKS? PAGE NINE

Front-page news

The front page of the *Daily Mirror* from 2nd December, 1976, describing the outrage by TV viewers following an interview of the Sex Pistols and other punks by Bill Grundy on an early-evening chat show. The punks, goaded by a drunken Grundy, spat out a series of obscenities. As a result, Grundy was suspended for two weeks and the programme was axed two months later.

2nd December, 1976

Malcolm in the middle
Malcolm McLaren, manager of the Sex Pistols, at a press conference in Manchester to defend the band against growing criticism of their recent television appearance on the *Today* programme.
2nd December, 1976

Sex and the single girl
Pamela Rooke, known as Jordan, at Malcolm McLaren's shop, Sex, on The King's Road, where she worked.
5th December, 1976

SEX

Punk emporium
Sex offered punk fashion, much of it designed by Vivienne Westwood.
5th December, 1976

Striking a pose
Jordan always cut a striking figure. She subsequently became Adam and The Ants' manager, although only for a short time.
5th December, 1976

New boy
After Glen Matlock left the Sex Pistols, following differences with Johnny Rotten, Sid Vicious (R) joined the line-up.
1st July, 1977

Ripping yarn
Ripped clothing was a staple of punk fashion. A run-in with the law added kudos to the bad-boy, anti-establishment image.
6th August, 1977

101 OLD CHURCH STREET

Punk poet
Patti Smith's work was an amalgamation of rock and poetry. She was also an artist and rock journalist.
11th May, 1976

Keeping his shirt on
American singer Iggy Pop, whose work with The Stooges in the early 1970s helped lay the foundations for the punk movement.
1st March, 1977

Clash bash

The Clash play a gig at the Students Union, Newcastle Upon Tyne: Mick Jones on guitar (L), Paul Simonon on bass (second L), Joe Strummer on guitar and vocals (C), and Nicky 'Topper' Headon on drums.
20th May, 1977

US pioneers
Blondie, fronted by singer Debbie Harry, were major contributors to the early American punk and New Wave scenes. They were regulars at the CBGB club in New York.
1st April, 1977

UK pioneers
The Damned, fronted by Dave Vanian (L), were the first UK punk band to release a single and an album, and to have a record in the UK charts.
10th April, 1977

Fashionistas
Punk fashion was wide ranging; even a string vest could be put to good use.
1st December, 1976

Debbie does punk
Debbie Wilson, an assistant in Malcolm McLaren's shop, Sex, wears an oversize coat, chiffon top and bondage trousers. Wilson adopted the name Debbie Juvenile and was a member of the 'Bromley Contingent', a group of Sex Pistols fans who were major innovators of early punk fashion.
December, 1977

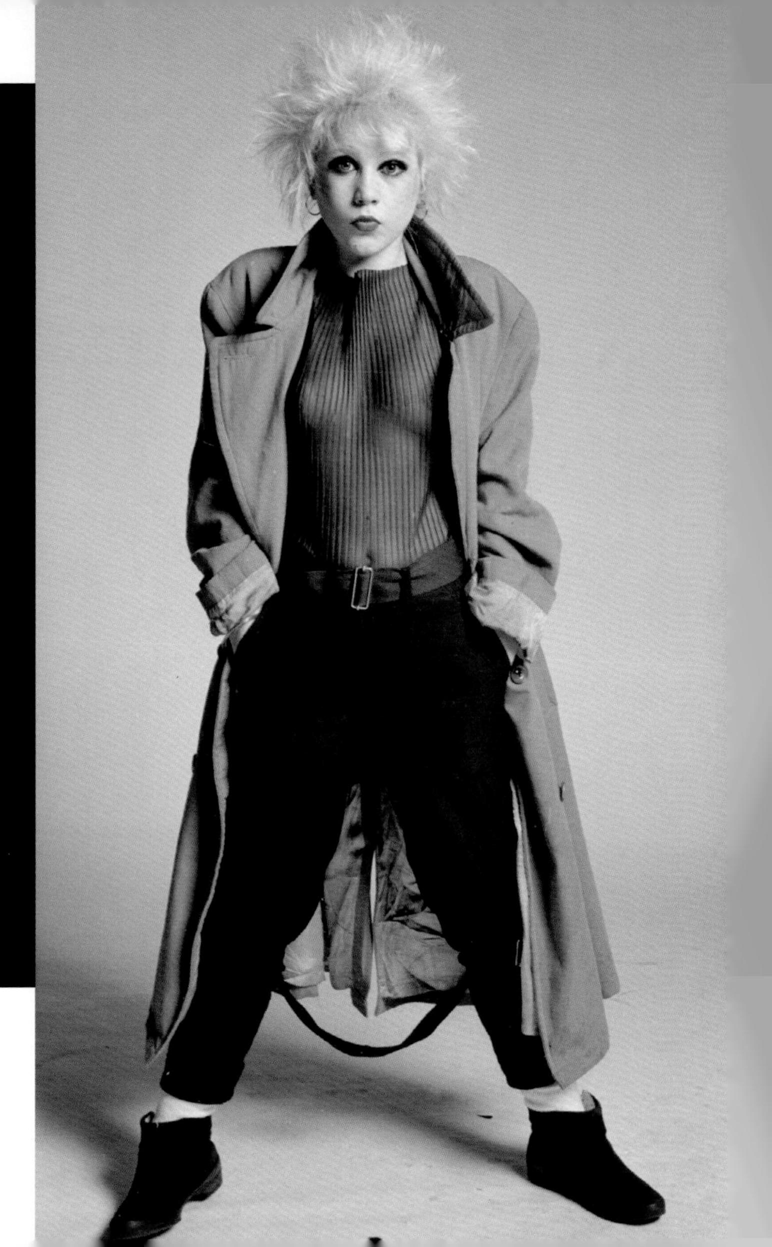

Camera shy?
The Sex Pistols play to the camera while on tour in the Netherlands.
December, 1977

Going Dutch
The Sex Pistols play a gig in Maasbree, Netherlands: Johnny Rotten (lead vocals), Sid Vicious (bass – background, far L), Steve Jones (guitar and backing vocals), Paul Cook (drums).
11th December, 1977

Holland daze
Sid Vicious looks out of it as the Sex Pistols play a gig at Maasbree in the Netherlands.
11th December, 1977

Taking it easy

Johnny Rotten (real name John Lydon) relaxes after the Maasbree gig.

11th December, 1977

Underneath the arches

The Stranglers in Manchester for a gig. L–R: Jet Black, Jean-Jacques Burnel, Hugh Cornwell, Dave Greenfield.

8th June, 1977

Rip it up! Fee Waybill, singer with American New Wave band The Tubes, adopts punk clothing and pins for a ripping time on stage.
29th April, 1978

Bad boys

After signing to A&M Records, having been dropped by EMI, the Sex Pistols gave a press conference at the company's offices. Intoxicated, they caused mayhem. Their antics over the following days caused further consternation among the company's executives, who broke the band's contract six days later. Some 25,000 copies of their new single, God Save The Queen, were destroyed before being released. Subsequently, they signed with Virgin, who released the single.

10th March, 1977

REGENT BAR
PJD 230E

Court appearance

Right: Joe Strummer (L) and Nicky Headon of The Clash, after appearing in court at Morpeth, charged with the theft of a pillowcase from the Holiday Inn hotel in Seaton Burn, North Tyneside. They were fined £100.
13th June, 1977

Low strummer
Left: Julian Isaacs, aka Auntie Pus, the punk balladier, demonstrates his playing style.
20th September, 1977

Strolling
A punk couple out for a stroll.
21st September, 1977.

MORON
ANTI
HERO
DON'T KNOW WHAT I WANT
BUT I KNOW HOW TO GET IT
I WANNA DESTROY THE PASSERBY
COS I WANNA BE ANARCHY
NO DOGSBODY
Save

Done to a T

Punk wearing a Sex Pistols T-shirt with a design based on the sleeve of their single, God Save the Queen.

8th July, 1977

Gone shopping
A fashionably dressed punk couple go shopping on the King's Road in London.
30th July, 1977

fighters

ols manager Malcolm McLaren and fashion designer Vivienne
od outside Bow Street Magistrates' Court, where they had been
ed on bail for fighting during the Sex Pistols' riverboat party.

:, 1977

GOD SAVE THE QUEEN
SHE AIN'T NO HUMAN BEING

Splashing out
Punks and teddy boys taunt each other outside a pub in London.
1st August, 1977

Spoiling for a fight
Punks gather in the King's Road, London, ready for another clash with teddy boys.
30th July, 1977

GRUNDY: Are they?
PISTOL: Yes they really turn us on. They do.
night . . . I'll be seeing you soon. I hope I'm not seeing YOU again. Goodnight.
turned into a shocker when Grundy asked about £40,000 that the Sex Pistols received
Grundy.
"You dirty f---er."
"What?"
WHO ARE THESE PUNKS?

Defiant gestures
Sex Pistols singer Johnny Rotten (L), with band manager Malcolm McLaren, leaves Malborough Street Magistrates' Court after being fined for possessing an illegal drug.
11th March, 1977

Street fashion

Civil servant Peter King (L) displays a more refined, less-aggressive type of punk fashion. The individual on the right is more confrontational, with chains, studs and leather fingerless gloves.
1977

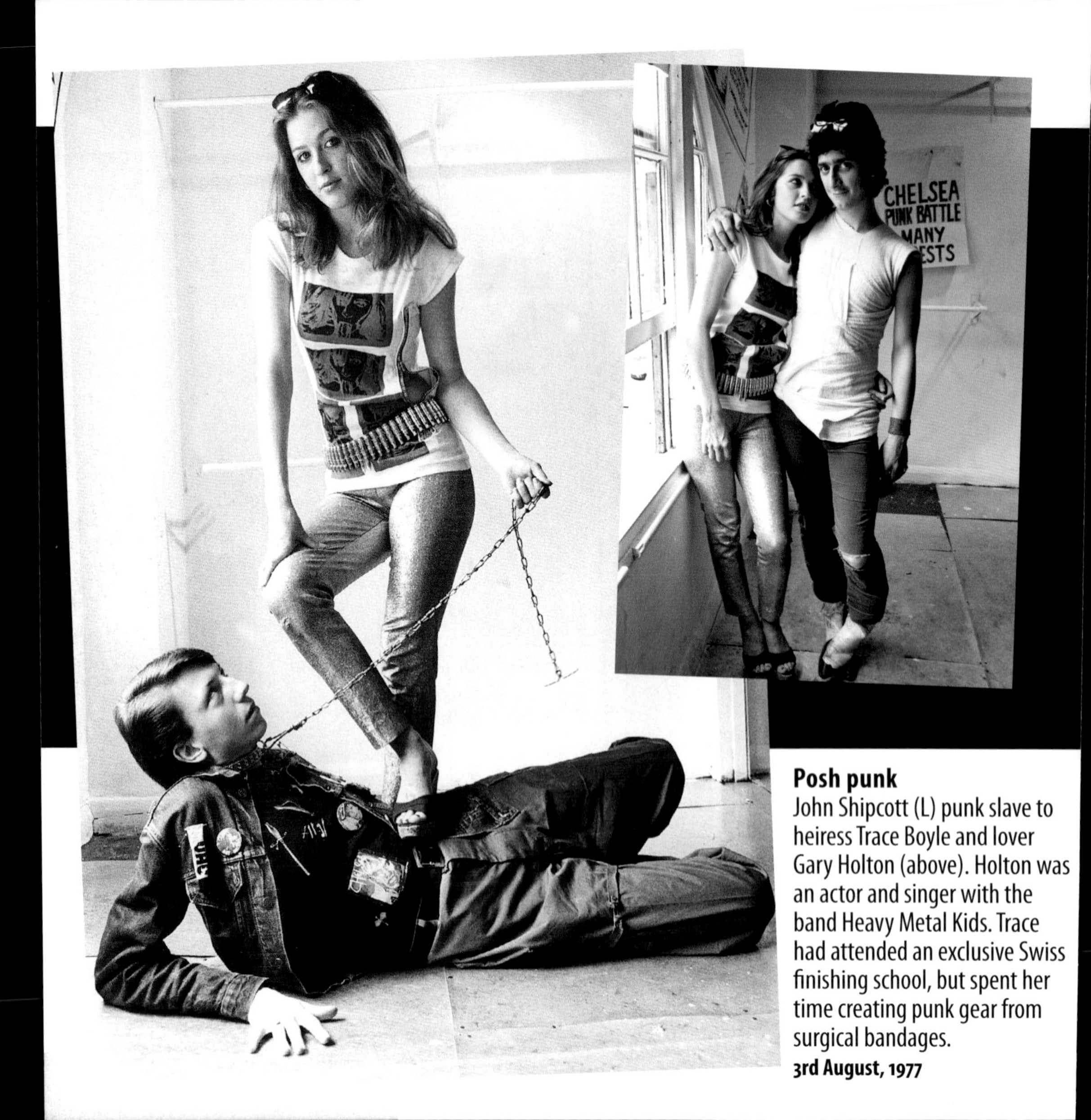

Posh punk
John Shipcott (L) punk slave to heiress Trace Boyle and lover Gary Holton (above). Holton was an actor and singer with the band Heavy Metal Kids. Trace had attended an exclusive Swiss finishing school, but spent her time creating punk gear from surgical bandages.
3rd August, 1977

Animal skins

Leather jackets and leopard-print materials were staples of punk street fashion.

18th December, 1977

Change of direction
Accountancy student Ian Hodge, from Woolwich in south London, who gave up studying to follow the punk lifestyle. His outfit combines some interesting items, including a gentleman's abdominal support.
12th June, 1977

Cheers!
This punk enjoys a beer in a pub at Woolwich in south London. Face and ear piercings were ideal for linking with chains.
12th June, 1977

Pinned up
As well as adorning clothes, the safety pin could be used with piercings to good effect – perhaps to link a chain from ear to mouth (L) or from ear to septum (R). Piercings may have been done professionally or self-inflicted.
12th June, 1977

Gone, gone, gone

Adoring fans watch the The Stranglers performing in Manchester on a warm summer night.

9th June, 1977

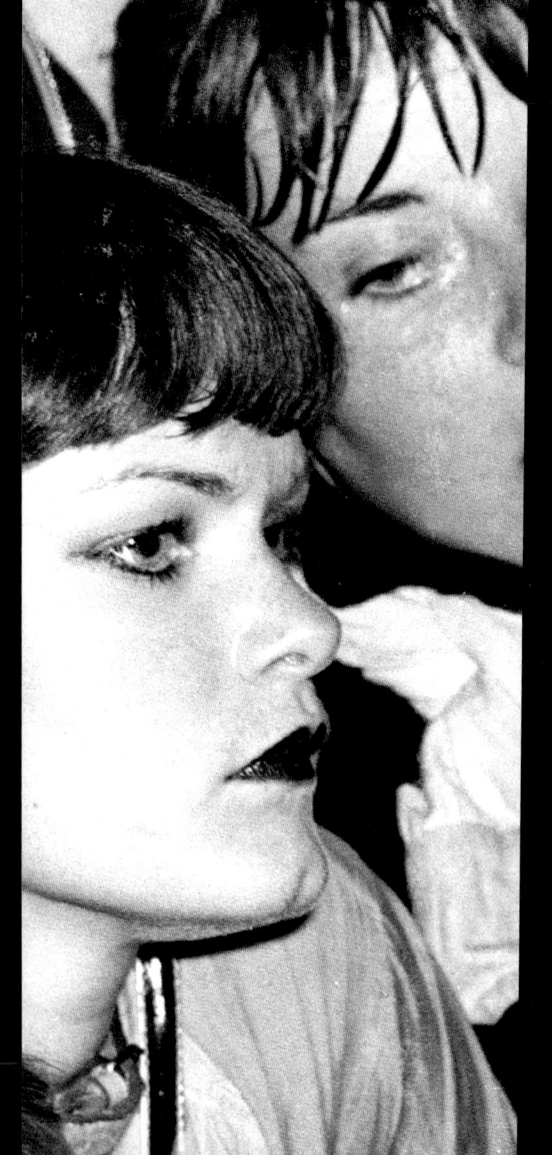

Punks plus

The age and musical skills of The Stranglers set them apart from the run of punk bands; even so, the band members considered themselves part of the punk movement.

9th June, 1977

Front men

Left: Jean-Jacques Burnel (L) and Hugh Cornwell front The Stranglers during their Manchester gig.

9th June, 1977

Singin' the blues?

Cornwell had been a blues musician before becoming a co-founder of The Stranglers in Guildford, Surrey, in 1974

9th June, 197

Clip art
Facing page: If safety pins were in short supply, paper clips would do.
12th June, 1977

Tragic case
Sid Vicious (real name John Ritchie), bass player with the Sex Pistols. Vicious would die of a drug overdose in New York, after being released on bail for the murder of his girlfriend, Nancy Spungen.
29th March, 1977

Punk predecessor Although not a punk musician himself, Ian Dury, best known for his work in the late 1970s with his band, The Blockheads, was considered as being protopunk for the influence his work had on early punk musicians.
6th December, 1977

VENUS

After a fashion

Punk icon Jordan and friend take part in a fashion shoot.

1977

GOD Save THE QUEEN
SEX PISTOLS

Shirt fronts

Shirts with contentious slogans were common in many punks' wardrobes. Here, tops bearing the sleeve image from the Sex Pistols' controversial single, God Save The Queen, are modelled by Jordan and friend.

1977

Seditious sentiment In early 1977, the Sex Pistols released the derogatory single God Save The Queen, the sleeve of which showed an image of Queen Elizabeth with her features obscured by the band and song names. Two versions of this image were applied to shirts sold in Malcolm McLaren's shop, now called Seditionaries. One had the features obscured (R), while the other showed the Queen with a safety pin through her upper lip (L).

1977

NO FUTURE
DOG
GOD SAVE THE
SEX PISTOLS
DIRT
YOU LOOK
PRETTY VACANT

A girl named Sioux
Left: Siouxsie Sioux (real name Susan Ballion) is considered to be one of the most influential singers of the rock era.
3rd December, 1976

Punk roots
Right: Although they would evolve musically, Siouxsie and The Banshees, fronted by Siouxsie Sioux, had their roots in the punk movement, having been inspired originally by the Sex Pistols.
1st October, 1978

Moving on

American New Wave band The Cars in London: L–R: Elliot Easton, Ric Ocasek, Greg Hawkes, David Robinson and Ben Orr. New Wave developed from punk rock, relying on much of its sound and spirit, and its predeliction for short, punchy songs.

16th November, 1978

Punk mum
Viva Hamnel, a 'lollipop lady' in Callington, Cornwall, also was a singer with her son's punk band.
1978

Pistols performance
The Sex Pistols on stage.
1978

On a charge
Sex Pistols bassist Sid Vicious with girlfriend Nancy Spungen at Marylebone Magistrates' Court on a drugs charge.
8th February, 1978

Lashing out
Sid Vicious reacts to being photographed at Marylebone Magistrates' Court, while Nancy Spungen descends the steps behind.
12th May, 1978

Supporting Sid

Gary Howe and Jane Hall model Sid Vicious T-shirts, sold by Malcolm McLaren through his Seditionaries shop in London to help support the Sex Pistols bassist, who had been arrested and charged with the murder of his girlfrend, Nancy Spungen, in New York.

October, 1978

Blonde having fun
Debbie Harry's blonde-bombshell looks made her an acceptable face of the punk movement.
August, 1978

Wailing Banshees
Siouxsie and The Banshees on stage. Sioux had formed the band with bassist Steven Severin. Although initially a punk band, they quickly evolved to the post-punk genre and became highly regarded for their musical audacity.
1978

Punk poseur
Right: Belgian punk singer [Pl]astic Bertrand, [wh]o was credited as the artist on [th]e international hit single *Ça Plane Pour Moi*. In reality, the song had been recorded by its composer, Lou Deprijck.
1978

[Tr]ans punk
[Le]ft: American [tra]nssexual [pu]nk singer and [ac]tress Wayne [(la]ter Jayne) [Co]unty, who [m]oved to London [in] 1977 and [fo]rmed a band [ca]lled the Electric [Ch]airs. She was [re]nowned for her [ou]trageous stage [an]tics and such [so]ngs as *Are You [M]an Enough To [Be] A Woman?*
[..]th September, [19]78

Regular contributor
Caroline Coon, political activist, artist and journalist, who became a regular on the punk scene, writing for the music press. She also created artworks for bands such as The Clash, whom she managed for a while.
7th March, 1978

Suitably attire
Right: Actress Jenn
Runacre arrives fo
the premiere of Derel
Jarman's punk film
Jubilee, at The Nev
Gate cinema, London
Runacre played a
time travelling Queer
Elizabeth I in the film
22nd February, 1978

Pogo Plastic

Plastic Bertrand, the Belgian punk who would sing while pogo dancing.
June, 1978

Road to ruin
Left: Sid Vicious injects himself with heroin. Within the year, he would be dead from a drugs overdose.
15th May, 1978

Where's Eddie?
Barry Masters, lead singer with Eddie and The Hot Rods, a band that spanned pub rock, punk rock and New Wave.
11th January, 1979

Rotten luck
Left: Johnny Rotten arrives at court on a drugs charge.
8th February, 1979

Fair cop?
Right: A police dog handler detains a pun wearing a 'Sid Vicious RIP' T-shirt.
27th August, 1979

SEX PISTOLS
SID
VICIOUS
RIP
BRIGADE

Forerunners
Protopunk band Ian Dury and The Blockheads in Cardiff for a gig. L–R: Davey Payne, John Turnbull, Ian Dury and Norman Watt-Roy.
1978

Coffin fit

Punk singer and actress Toyah Willcox. While attempting to establish her musical career, she lived in a converted British Rail warehouse in Battersea, London, which also acted as a studio. For want of a bed, she slept in a French Red Cross coffin.

1979

Deep in thought
Left: Punk singer Wayne County arrives for the premiere of Derek Jarman's film, *Jubilee*, in which she starred.
22nd February, 1978

At the pictures
Striking as ever, Jordan arrives with a friend for the premiere of Derek Jarman's punk film, *Jubilee*, in which she starred.
22nd February, 1978

Odd trio
Seen at the Women of the Year lunch: (L–R) author Jackie Collins, Poly Styrene (real name Marianne Elliott-Said), founder of punk band X-Ray Spex, and actress Carol Channing.
29th October, 1979

DICK
ALLEN GARFIELD
DEAN

No sham

Jimmy Pursey, founder and front man of the punk band Sham 69, which would have a major influence on the Oi! movement. Sham 69 had a large skinhead following, and their gigs were often peppered with violence. Indeed, the band stopped performing live after a 1978 gig was broken up by fighting among white-power skinheads.
26th March, 1979

All tied up

Bondage jackets and trousers, created by Vivienne Westwood and sold through Seditionaries in London, allowed punks to make an anti-fashion statement.

1977

TARTAN

Prince of punks?
Prince Charles chats with a group of punks who turned up to watch him at a polo match.
27th May, 1979

Blown away
UK Subs, one of the earliest British punk bands: (L–R) Charlie Harper (vocals), Pete Davies (drums) and Nicky Garratt (guitar).
14th September, 1979

Old-age punk
Len Lacey of Northwich, Cheshire, with his punk album, *This is Life*.
12th September, 1979.

No angels
Left: Punk/Oi! band Angelic Upstarts. Their debut single, *The Murder of Liddle Towers*, is considered one of the best punk rock singles of all time.
31st August, 1979

Punk pioneers
Right: The Stranglers, among the instigators of the British punk rock scene.
February, 1979

THE
POLICE

Police men
Above: Stewart Copeland wanted his new band to be part of the burgeoning punk scene, but The Police ended up as one of the first New Wave bands, their music influenced by punk, reggae and jazz. L–R: Copeland, Sting, Andy Summer.
2nd January, 1980

Gigging
Left: The Police play a gig.
1st October, 1981

Go girls

Formed as a punk band on the LA scene in the United States in 1978, the Go-Go's included among their number Belinda Carlisle (top R), who adopted the name Dottie Danger. By 1982, the band had moved away from punk into the New Wave and pop rock genres.

August, 1982

Misspent youth?
Louise Goodall, actress, pictured in her youth when she was a punk.
1980

Comparing views
A priest and some punks in debate after listening to speeches at the Durham Miners Gala.
1980

Remembering Sid

Punks march in London to mark the first anniversary of Sid Vicious's death.

3rd February, 1980

On the march
Punks gather in London to remember Sid Vicious.
3rd February, 1980

Biker gear

Leather biker jackets adorned with studs, badges and slogans were synonymous with punk fashion.
3rd February, 1980

ANARCHY IN '79

Head cases

Apart from unconventional clothing, eye-catching hairstyles and colours were important means of punk self-expression.

3rd February, 1980

Hair piece
Early punks commonly cropped their hair and made it look messy or dyed it unnatural colours. Later, the Mohican – Mohawk in the USA (R) – began to gain favour.
3rd February, 1980

Sex PISTOLS
BELSEN WAS A GAS

Gathering at the square

Some of the 300 or so punks who gathered at Sloane Square in London to mark the first anniversary of the death of Sex Pistols bass guitarist Sid Vicious. Clothing adorned with provocative slogans help foster the punks' anti-establishment image, although whether the sentiments expressed were genuine is debatable.

3rd February, 1980

SID LIVES

Long live Sid

Punks at Sloane Square, London, remember Sid Vicious and tease the photographer.

3rd February, 1980

Tartan terror?
Tartan was another popular material with punks, who often wore short kilts over bondage trousers.
3rd February, 1980

Pin-up punk
Beki Bondage (real name Rebecca Bond) was considered Britain's first punk pin-up, having appeared in a number of influential music magazines. The singer/songwriter/guitarist was a founding member of punk band Vice Squad.
2nd December, 1982

Paper hanger
Hugh Cornwell, vocalist with The Stranglers, contemplates a little wallpapering.
21st January, 1982

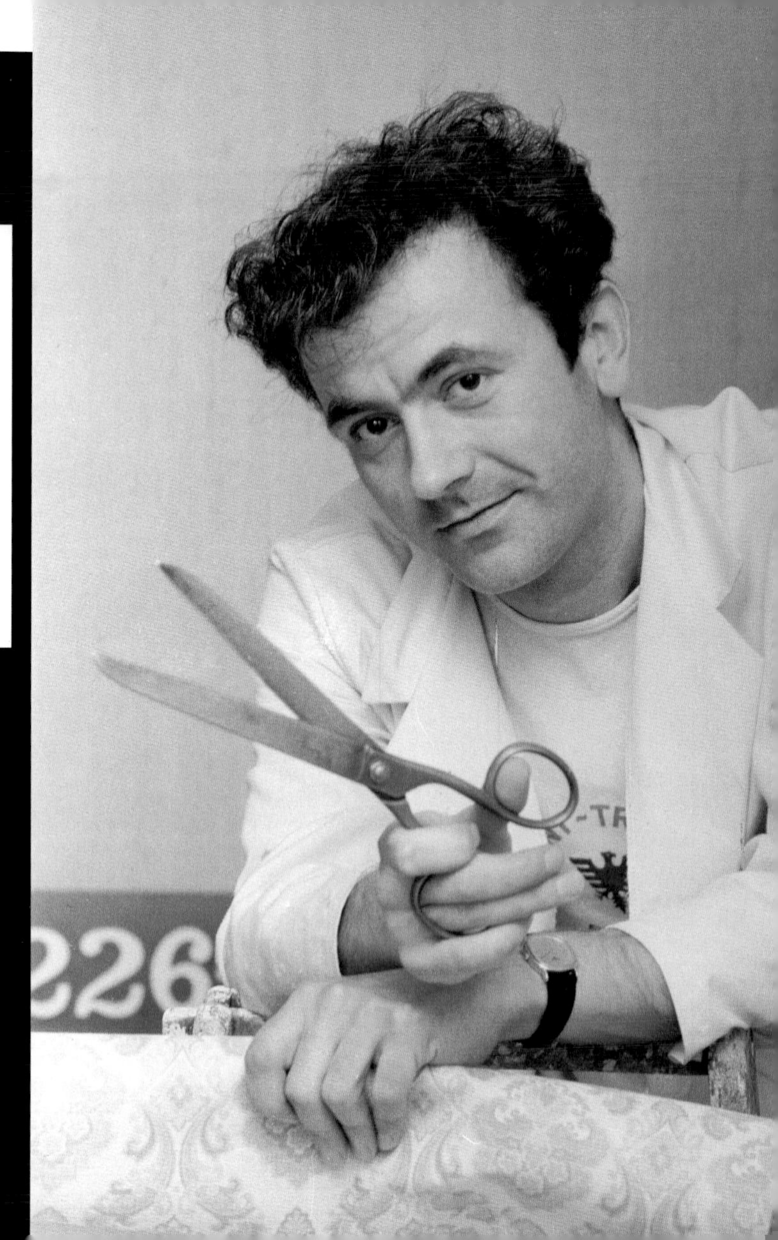

Cat hair

Punk Nigel Smith gets a cheetah hairdo.

25th May, 1980

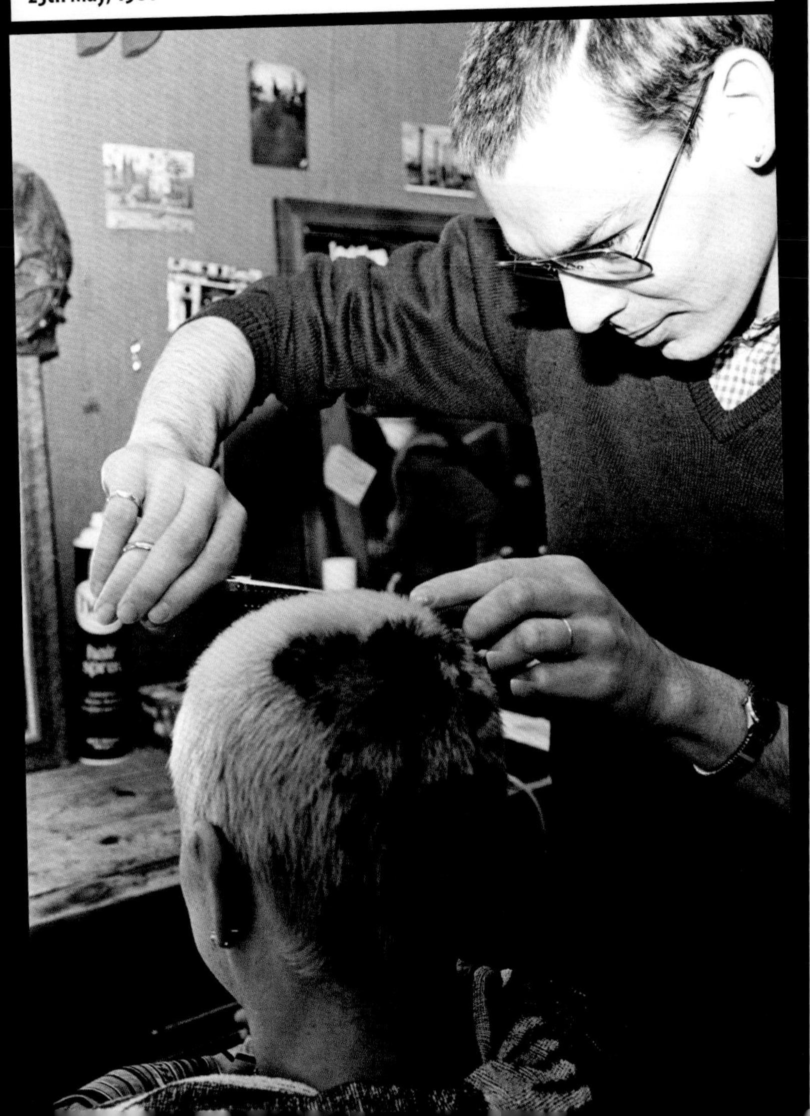

Long and the short
A dramatic combination of cropped and long hair.
1980

Shocking spikes
Right: Spiked hair for both men and women became increasingly popular and often reached extreme lengths. All intended to shock, which it did.
27th March, 1983

Watching the world go by
A punk with spiked hair takes time out on a park bench.
September, 1983

New collaboration

Former Sex Pistol John Lydon (R) with songwriter and musician Keith Levene. Lydon had left the Pistols in 1978 and, with Levene, formed Public Image Ltd, arguably the first post-punk band.

18th March, 1981

Fashion shoot
Right: Magazine take on punk fashion: black T-shirt with zips, spray-pattern bondage trousers, black inspector jacket with zips and studded belt.
September, 1983

Going mainstream
Centre right: Toyah Willcox began to move away from her punk roots, but the dramatic hair remained.
5th September, 1983

Going solo
Far right: Billy Idol, originally a member of punk band Generation X, enjoyed further success as a solo artist.
1st August, 1980

Devoted couple
To show their devotion, this punk couple chained themselves together using their nose piercings.
10th April, 1981

Strange mate
Steve Strange and friend Perry. Strange (real name Steven Harrington) eschewed his punk roots to form the New Wave band Visage, adopting the New Romantic look.
1981

Tying the knot
David Bancroft and Alison Wyn-de-Bank celebrate their punk wedding with friends and family at Bletchley, Milton Keynes.
25th October, 1980

Colourful pair
Right: Startling hair colours, leather jackets, leopard print and tartan: all great ingredients of the punk look.
1981

Close shave
Left: Gary Lambadarios won a battle for his job after his flame-coloured Mohican haircut made bosses see red at a television factory in South Wales. Union chiefs went on the warpath when the 18-year-old was ordered to axe the Mohican or join the dole queue.
4th May, 1985

Skids row
The Scottish band Skids perform an outdoor gig in Brighton, Sussex.
16th October, 1980

Ant eater
Below: Although recognised now as one of the New Romantics, Adam Ant (real name Stuart Goddard) began his career in the burgeoning punk movement.
1980

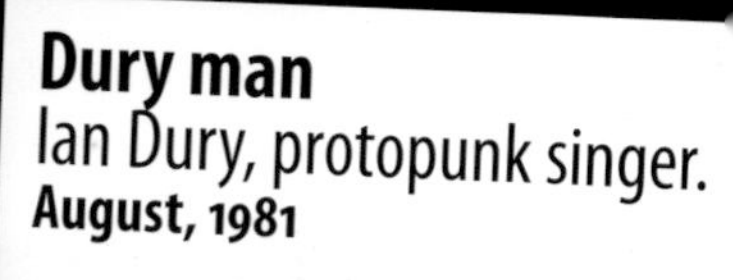

Dury man
Ian Dury, protopunk singer.
August, 1981

Band not a board

Below: Punk band 4 Be 2 counted John Lydon's younger brother, Jimmy (C), among its founding members. Some of the band would go on to form The Bollock Brothers.

November, 1980

Derry five
Below: The Undertones began as a punk band, (L–R) Michael Bradley, Feargal Sharkey, Billy Doherty, Damian O'Neill, John O'Neill.
15th May, 1980

Publicity stunt
Above: Michael Fagan (C), Buckingham Palace intruder, with punk band The Bollock Brothers. Fagan featured on the band's electro version of the Sex Pistols' album, *Never Mind The Bollocks*.
27th April, 1983

Broken up
Above: Coventry band The Wild Boys, who finally broke up in 1981.
16th October, 1981

Pilchards and bums
Right: Splodgenessabounds play a gig in Nottingham. Characterised as 'punk pathetiques', the band injected humour into its act, singing about pilchards and bums, unlike other Oi! bands, who addressed serious working-class issues, like the dole.
21st March, 1981

Tucking in
Left: Scottish punk band The Exploited enjoy a light snack.
November, 1980

Ready to rock
Right: Punk band with their amps crammed into someone's front room.
1980

Punks in the park

Kilts, both full-length and short, became a favourite form of dress among punks, who wore them over tartan or other trousers. A bum flap was a popular addition to a pair of bondage trousers.

30th March, 1980

Punk portrayal
Left: Adrian Edmondson, who played violent punk student Vyvyan in the TV sitcom *The Young Ones*. Edmondson's portrayal included a studded forehead – a step too far perhaps for even the most ardent of punks.
April, 1982

Trick of the trade
Right: Hairdresser Sharon McArthur displays her exotic punk hairstyle.
13th October, 1984

NO POPE
NO WELCOME TO BRITAIN

Punk protest
Punks gather for a march to protest at the Pope's forthcoming visit to Britain.
17th April, 1982

Rumble at Sarfend
Punks and skinheads cause trouble at Southend, Essex.
12th April, 1982

Hair today... Tesco worker Dave Liddle considers his options after being told he had a choice between his haircut and his job.
28th April, 1983

They mattered

The Clash: (L–R) Paul Simonon, Nicky Headon, Joe Strummer, Mick Jones. In their heyday, they were known as 'the only band that matters'.

21st April, 1982

Party punks

The Ace fashion shop in the King's Road, Chelsea holds a party for its showbiz clients, among them (L–R) Steve Strange, Billy Idol and Paul Tok.

25th September, 1982

Topknots
Maria Perez shows off her crowning glory and striking eye make-up.
10th April, 1981

Sweethearts

Punks Brian McEnaney (15) and girlfriend Lesley Smith (24) are separated by the school fence.

30th December, 1981

Short back and sides
Left: Sean Hewitson from Newbiggin, Northumberland, proudly wears his Mohican hairstyle.
March, 1984

Spikes and studs
Right: James O'Donald, from Glasgow, seen in the King's Road, Chelsea. His hair is in the classic spiked Mohican style.
March, 1983

Hair raiser
Far right: Janet Lazard's amazing hair.
January, 1985

Platinum blonde
Left: Debbie Harry, singer with the American punk/New Wave band Blondie.
18th March, 1984

Book launch
Right: Debbie Harry and Chris Stein, co-founders of Blondie, at a party to celebrate publication of *Making Tracks – The Rise of Blondie*.
20th May, 1982

Stand-ups

Even relatively short hair could be turned into a Mohican or a series of random spikes with the aid of soap or gel.

1980

Jamming
Paul Weller of The Jam during a gig in Brighton, Sussex. The band spanned the gamut of punk, New Wave and mod revival.
12th December, 1982

Mystery girl
Toyah Willcox performing at the Rock and Pop Awards.
24th February, 1982

ıa Hanson becomes a model for her father, Madame Tussaud's wax museum in London.

Nice boys

Adam and The Ants in their 'dandy highwaymen' days, having left the punk scene behind. This photo was taken at The Palladium in Hollywood, USA, where Adam would be voted the 'sexiest man in America' by viewers of MTV.
December, 1982

On the Beeb
Toyah Willcox moved steadily away from the punk scene, although she retained her flame-coloured hair (R). She developed her acting career, appearing in the BBC comedy *Dear Heart* (L).
1982

Tomboy?
Many punk girls eschewed feminine clothing in favour of an androgynous look.
29th March, 1983

Punk icon
Joe Strummer (real name John Mellor) of The Clash, considered to be one of the most iconic figures of the punk movement.
16th January, 1981

Variation on a style
Left: Mohican hairstyles could be very narrow or much broader with only the sides of the head shaved, like that of geography student Andrew Askins from Penrith, Cumbria.
27th April, 1983

Nice hair
Right: The Prince of Wale chats to punks Beverley Scott (L) and Mary Murra at Consett during a tour the Northeast.
22nd October, 1984

Idol worship
Billy Idol in concert on Long Island, New York, USA.
11th September, 1984

Solo success

Billy Idol moved to New York after Generation X disbanded in 1981. There he pursued a successful solo career.

11th September, 1984

Sioux Who?

Right: Guitarist Pete Townsend of The Who and Siouxsie Sioux attend the launch of an anti-drug campaign.

19th April, 1985

Prince's pair

Far right: Punk couple Sharlene Burnell and Gary Telford, who were photographed by Prince Andrew for a calendar.

5th April, 1984

Scrubs up nice

The two sides of Captain Sensible, co-founder of The Damned.

1983

Pet sounds
Captain Sensible at home with Rabbit, his pet rabbit.
13th June, 1984

Only human
New Wave band Human League, fronted by vocalist Philip Oakey (second L). They favoured the New Romantic style, but their work still had elements of punk rock.
17th May, 1982

Making a statement
Right: Messed up, coloured hair made an anti-establishment statement.
1985

Acting up
Punks play to the camera.
1985

Pucker punk
Left: A policeman receives a kiss from a girl punk in Trafalgar Square, London on New Year's Eve.
1st January, 1984

Lost punk
Policemen outside the Bank of England direct a punk demonstrator to the Stop the City protest.
27th September, 1984

Paving the way
Left: Lee Brilleaux of pub rock band Dr Feelgood. The band's hard, R&B-influenced rock'n'roll paved the way for punk bands like The Stranglers.
30th August, 1981

Velvet Lou
Right: American singer/songwriter Lou Reed, formerly a member of The Velvet Underground, also had an influence on early punk musicians.
31st March, 1987

Not pretending
Left: Chrissie Hynde on stage. Hynde had been involved with several unsuccessful punk bands before forming The Pretenders in 1978.
1982

Cramps Interior
Lux Interior (real name Erick Purkhiser), singer with American band The Cramps.
20th April, 1986

Act of charity
Grandmother Lil Bone dressed as a punk to raise money for charity.
12th July, 1980

Post-Pistols
Malcolm McLaren, after his time as manager of the Sex Pistols, displays sartorial elegance.
13th August, 1985

Mohican max
Left: Rebecca Malpass eyeball-to-eyeball with punk model Matt Belgrano.
19th December, 1986

I'll show you mine…
Punks Wendy Darlow and boyfriend Martyn Hawden compare hairstyles.
9th April, 1985

Beasties
Left: Although they came to prominence as a hip-hop band, America's Beastie Boys started out as a hardcore pun band in 1981.
1983

Glam drummer
Right: Ray Mayhew, drumme and vocalist with the glam punk band Sigue Sigue Sputnik, which had been formed by bassist Tony Jame previously with Generation X
1984

Heading for orbit
Glam punk band Sigue Sigue Sputnik in concert. The band had been formed by former Generation X bassist Tony James (L) and included Neal X (R).
28th February, 1986

Spaced-out odyssey
A dazed looking fan is helped from the stage by Sigue Sigue Sputnik keyboard player Yana (L), while vocalist Martin Degville lets rip (below).
28th February, 1986

Punk patriots
A group of punks show a variety of Mohican hairstyles and demonstrate their patriotic feelings.
23rd July, 1986

Tribute band
Right: The Scottish Sex Pistols, who released an album in 1983 titled *Never Mind The Trossachs Here's The Scottish Sex Pistols*.
1983

Fender PRECISION BASS

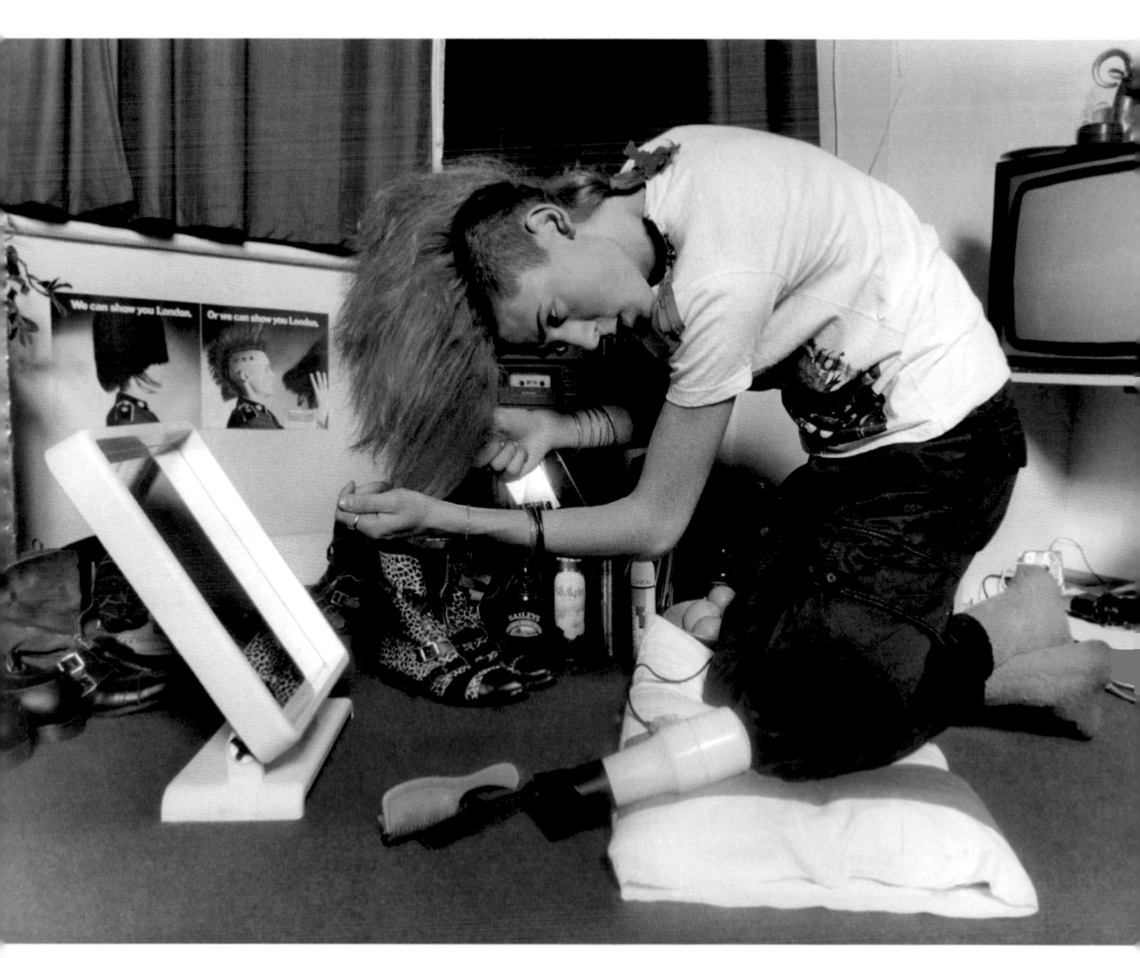

Keeping up appearances

Punk model Matt Belgrano gets to work on his hair, before a photo shoot at Big Ben in London.

April, 1986

Originators
American band The Ramones play a gig at The Ritz in New York, USA, during which fans dive from the stage into the crowd (inset). The Ramones are often cited as the first punk rock band, and despite limited success, they had a major influence on the punk rock movement on both sides of the Atlantic.
11th September, 1987

What's in a name?
The Ramones on stage at the Reading Rock Festival. From their early days, all the members of the band changed their surname to Ramone. Dee Dee Ramone (real name Douglas Colvin) played bass (L), while Joey Ramone (Jeffry Hyman) was lead vocalist.
1st August, 1988

TAMA
Marshall

Rooftop gig
Left: Echo and The Bunnymen, a post-punk band, play a gig on a London rooftop. Post-punk bands, with their roots in punk, produced a sound that was less pop orientated than that of New Wave bands.
6th July, 1987

Demonstrator
Right: Singer/songwriter Billy Bragg at an anti-Gulf War demonstration with Labour politician Ken Livingstone (behind). A left-wing activist, Bragg was the most successful proponent of folk punk with a string of hits during the 1980s.
21st January, 1991

Youthful expression
Well-known actress and model Elizabeth Hurley was a punk in her late teens and dressed the part. She also dyed her hair pink.
1984

Rotten wife
John Lydon and wife Nora, a publishing heiress from Germany.
24th September, 1989

Short contract

Left: Fur (real name Jennifer Dixon), bass player with The Cramps. She remained with the band for only two months while on a world tour.
20th April, 1986

Prime movers

American band The Cramps: (L–R) Nick Knox, Fur, Poison Ivy, Lux Interior. Poison Ivy (real name Kristy Wallace) and Lux Interior were husband and wife, and they were the founding members of the band. One of the first garage punk bands, The Cramps were among the prime innovators of the psychobilly genre and also inspired many goth rock bands.
20th April, 1986

Irish pioneers
Left: Shane MacGowan of The Pogues, an Irish band that pioneered folk punk, a fusion of traditional folk music with punk rock. In 1987, they had a UK No. 2 single with *Fairytale of New York*, a collaboration with Kirsty McColl (background).
11th March, 1988

Damned David
Above: David Vanian, vocalist with The Damned.
1st June, 1988

:xplosive combination
'unk styles even entered the mainstream. Dance trio TNT adopted fetish gear and vivid make-up.
980

Brolly head
Mike 'The Spike' Lang added a twist to his Mohican haircut with tiny cocktail umbrellas.
4th March, 1981

Drink up or I shoot!
A punk with a striking Mohican hairstyle fools around with a child's cap pistol, while her companion concentrates on finishing his beer.
15th January, 1988

MILK

One too many?
Right: While his companion tries to help him to his feet, this punk vents his anger on the photographer.
15th January, 1988

Extension pieces
Far right: A Mohican with side wings.
15th January, 1988

Earnest discussion
The floor is as good as anywhere to hold a conversation. The girls in this group show a propensity for fetish boots; fishnet tights were also a staple of punk female fashion.
15th January, 1988

Haircut 100

A punk at the 100 Club on Oxford Street, London to commemorate the tenth anniversary of the final Sex Pistols concert in San Francisco in 1978.

15th January, 1988

Film maker
Facing page: Derek Jarman, English film director, who was responsible for the UK's first punk movie, *Jubilee*, released in 1978, which many regard as his first masterpiece. It featured many punk groups and figures, including Wayne County, Toyah Willcox, Jordan, and Adam and The Ants.
24th March, 1988.

Smiling Rotten
Left: John Lydon contemplates the release of his band Public Image Ltd's latest album, *9*.
1989

Record sale

American band The Ramones at the Oxford Street, London HMV Music Store to promote their first compilation album, *Ramones Mania*. Photo right shows (L–R) Johnny Ramone, Joey Ramone and Dee Dee Ramone.
18th June, 1988

RAMONES

Men in black
The Stranglers, minus founding member Hugh Cornwell, who had left to pursue a solo career. L–R: Jean-Jacques Burnel, Paul Roberts, Jet Black, Dave Greenfield, John Ellis.
10th January, 1991

Singing cure
Right: Robert Smith, lead singer of post-punk/New Wave band The Cure. Since the band's inception in 1976, Smith has been the sole constant member.
23rd April, 1992

A long way from punk
Vivienne Westwood, award winning fashion designer, at the Swatch shop in Oxford Street, London, to launch her watch, The Orb.
18th April, 1993

Acting the part
Toyah Willcox, now an established actress, would play the part of Miss Scarlett in a television *Cluedo* programme to be screened on Boxing Day, 1990.
29th November, 1990

Sex

Pistols in the park
A fan tussles with security men during a gig by the re-formed Sex Pistols at Finsbury Park, London, part of their Filthy Lucre Tour.
23rd June, 1996

Saluted
A punk at the Sex Pistols gig in Finsbury Park, London shows her appreciation of the camera.
23rd June, 1996

Hairstyles
Johnny Rotten (John Lydon) displays two distinctly different styles of coiffure during the re-formed Sex Pistols' Filthy Lucre Tour. The Phoenix Festival at Long Marston Airfield, near Stratford-upon-Avon, saw the red and yellow number (L), while fans at Finsbury Park, London, were treated to the pale blue spikes.
1996

McEWAN'S
EXHIBITION
EXHIBITION
INNESS
McEWAN'S

Oi!, Oi!
Left: Mensi (real name Thomas Mensforth), vocalist with the punk/Oi! band Angelic Upstarts, behind the bar of his own country pub.
1990

Police doctor
Right: Sting receives an honorary doctorate of music from the University of Northumbria.
13th November, 1992

Three stiffs
Irish punk band Stiff Little Fingers in their later years: (L–R) Bruce Foxton (bass), Jake Burns (vocals), Dolphin Taylor (drums).
1994

Blood brothers
Punk band Bleed: (L–R) Andrew Duncan (drums), Greg Robson (guitar), Mark Watson (bass).
11th June, 1998

Knife charge
Chrissie Hynde (R) at Uxbridge Magistrates' Court, where she appeared on a charge of attempting to board a plane at Heathrow carrying a banned knife. She was acquitted.
21st March, 1997

Part of the Establishment
Right: Vivienne Westwood at 10 Downing Street for a party held by Prime Minister Tony Blair.
30th July, 1997

Hip-hopper

Malcolm McLaren in Glasgow to promote his hip-hop album, *Buffalo Gals Back 2 Skool*.

21st September, 1998

Czech mates

The Sex Pistols while on tour in Prague, Czech Republic.

9th July, 1996

Buzzers

English punk band China Drum riding their buzzboards, which attracted the displeasure of the police. L–R: Jan Alkema, Dave McQueen, Adam Lee, Bill McQueen. The band was active between 1989 and 2001.

29th May, 1997

Punks on parade
A national celebration of Queen Elizabeth the Queen Mother's 100th birthday included a pageant that took place on Horse Guards Parade, London, and that featured a group of punks.
19th July, 2000

Passage of time
The Sex Pistols showing their age.
6th July, 2002

Fiery performance
Billy Joe Armstrong of American pop punk band Green Day on stage during the T in the Park music festival at Kinross in Scotland.
14th July, 2002

On the waterfront
Left: Debbie Harry in concert with a re-formed Blondie at the Waterfront Hall, Belfast.
10th November, 2003

Rotten angry
Right: John Lydon vents his ire on the photographer during a boat trip at Surfers Paradise, Queensland. Lydon was in Australia for the making of the TV programme *I'm a Celebrity… Get Me Out of Here!*
7th February, 2004

Getting it back together
The re-united Skids rehearse in a recording studio.
4th May, 2002

Sitting the roof
Skids take time out to pose on the roof of the recording studio.
4th May, 2002

CHAOS U.K

Seeing pink
Iain Duncan Smith, at the time leader of the Conservative Party, chats with punk Nicholas Brooke during a visit to a factory in Blackpool, Lancashire.
8th October, 2003

Punk pastiche
A modern fashion editor's take on punk style: not quite the shock tactics employed by real punks.
22nd October, 2003

JUST A
LOVE&
Girl !

Jumping James
Left: James Bourne of pop punk band Busted, on stage during the Pepsi Silver Clef Concert in Manchester.
14th May, 2003

In the mainstream
Right: Tom Fletcher on stage in Newcastle with pop punk band McFly. Pop punk bands have brought punk into the mainstream by combining elements of the genre with pop music.
27th March, 2011

Poptastic

Left: Often characterised as the 'Godfather of punk', Iggy Pop contemplates the Living Legend Award presented to him by Classic Rock magazine.

1st November, 2009

Punk legends

Right: Tony James, formerly of Generation X and Sigue Sigue Sputnik, on stage at the Isle of White Festival as part of Carbon/Silicon, a rock duo he formed with ex-Clash guitarist Mick Jones.

2007

Fashion icon
Left: Vivienne Westwood accepts the applause for her Red Label Spring/ Summer Collection during London Fashion Week.
September, 2008

Rotten teeth
Right: John Lydon hams it up for the camera, although the state of his teeth was the reason for his stage name, Johnny Rotten. In 2008, he would undergo dental work in the USA costing around $22,000.
17th July, 2002

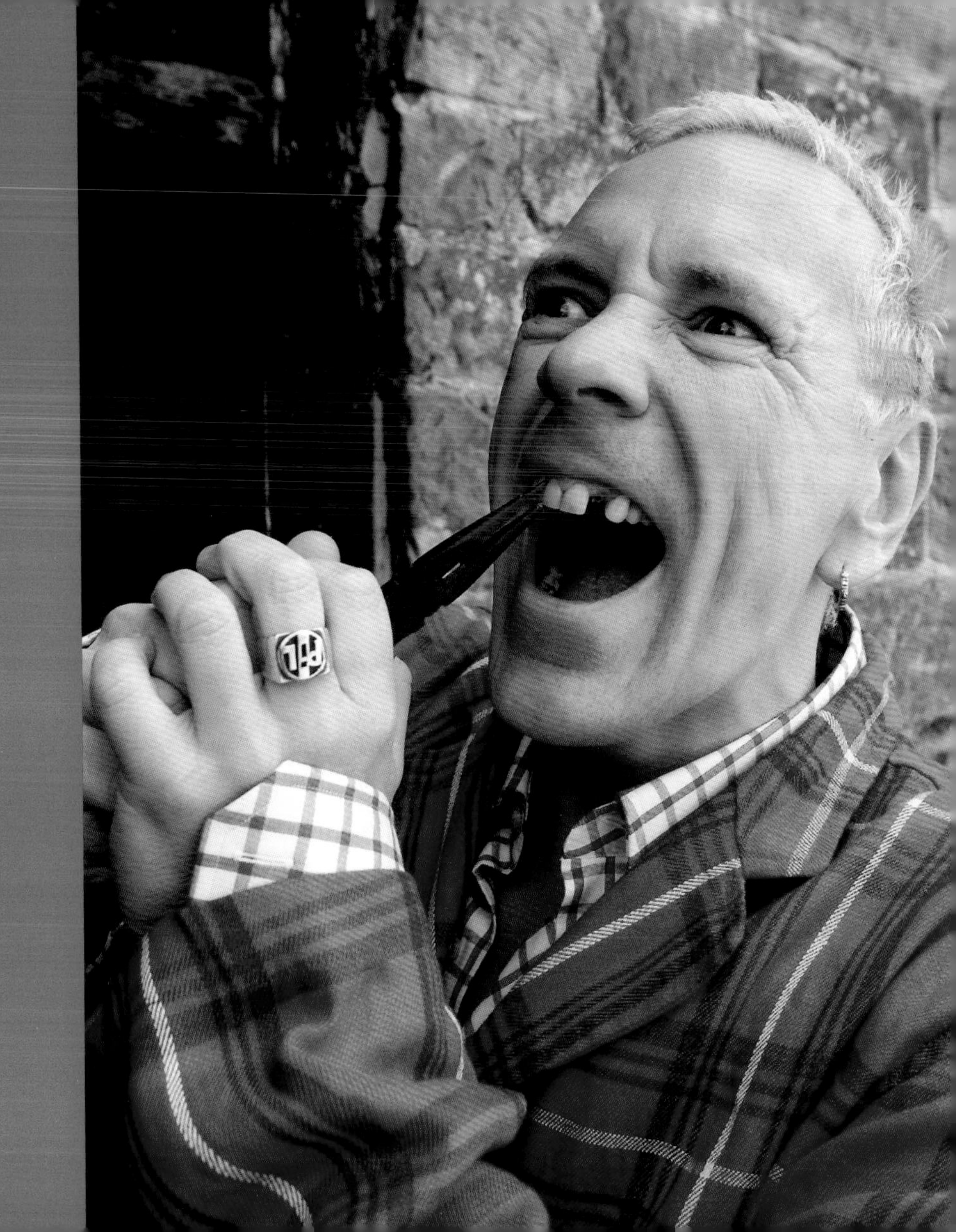

Reformed character

John Lydon encourages the crowd while on stage with the re-formed Sex Pistols at the Isle of Wight Festival.
2008

The publishers gratefully acknowledge Mirrorpix, from whose extensive archives
the photographs in this book have been selected.